Table of Co

Table of Content 1

Chapter 1: Introduction 2

Chapter 2: Early British Monarchs 6

Chapter 3: Tudor Dynasty 13

Chapter 4: Hanoverian Kings 19

Chapter 5: Windsors through the 20th Century 26

Chapter 6: Current Generation 32

Chapter 7: Royal Family Tree 39

Chapter 8: Royal Scandals and Controversies 45

Chapter 9: Royal Traditions and Ceremonies 52

Chapter 10: Conclusion 58

Chapter 1: Introduction

Importance of genealogy in understanding British history

One of the main benefits of genealogy in understanding British history is its ability to provide a more comprehensive view of political developments. Monarchies, for example, were long-standing institutions in British history. By tracing the lineage of kings and queens, we can observe patterns in succession and the impact of familial connections on political power. The Wars of the Roses, a pivotal period in British history, were rooted in competing claims to the throne by the houses of York and Lancaster. Genealogy sheds light on the complex web of family ties and inheritance disputes that ultimately shaped the outcome of this conflict.

Furthermore, genealogy allows us to comprehend the social dynamics of different periods in British history. By exploring our own family roots, we gain a sense of how our ancestors fit into the wider social hierarchy. Understanding the positions our ancestors held in society, whether as landowners, merchants, or farmers, provides a glimpse into the socio-economic structures prevailing in the past. By extrapolating this knowledge to broader society, we can better understand the divisions and interactions between classes during significant periods, such as the Industrial Revolution or the rise of the middle class.

In addition to providing historical context, genealogy contributes to a more nuanced understanding of cultural and artistic movements. For instance, the English Romantic poets of the 18th and 19th centuries, including William Wordsworth and Samuel Taylor Coleridge, were deeply influenced by their connections to the Lake District. By exploring genealogical records, we can identify their familial ties to this region and understand how their experiences there shaped their artistic expression. Understanding the backgrounds of prominent figures in art, literature, and music allows us to appreciate their creations in a richer historical and cultural context.

Genealogy also highlights the importance of migration and global connections that have shaped British history. The British Empire, one of the largest in history, spanned the globe and brought together people from diverse backgrounds. By exploring our own family histories, we may discover ties to regions and cultures beyond Britain. This realization challenges the notion of a singular British identity and underscores the multicultural nature of our country. Understanding the ancestral connections to other parts of the world deepens our appreciation for the richness and diversity of British history.

Beyond personal curiosity and historical perspective, genealogy plays a vital role in establishing and preserving national heritage. Family archives, old photographs, and personal documents all contribute to our collective memory. By digitizing and sharing these valuable resources, we ensure their accessibility to future generations. In doing so, we build a more comprehensive understanding of our shared history as a nation, connecting people across the country and fostering a sense of national identity. Its ability to shed light on political, social, and cultural aspects provides a comprehensive view of the forces that shaped our nation. Through the exploration of family lineage, we gain insight into the dynamics of power, social structures, artistic movements, and connections to the wider world. Furthermore, genealogy contributes to the preservation of national heritage by capturing personal stories and making them accessible to future generations. By embracing genealogy, we not only enrich our personal understanding of our ancestors but also contribute to a deeper, more nuanced understanding of British history as a whole.

Overview of the British monarchy

The British monarchy's origins can be traced back to the 9th century with the Anglo-Saxon kings. However, it was the Norman Conquest in 1066 that solidified the monarchy as we know it today. Since then, the crown has been passed down through inheritance, following complex rules of succession. Currently, Queen Elizabeth II reigns as the longest-serving monarch in British history, having ascended to the throne in 1952.

The monarchy operates within a constitutional framework, which means that its powers are limited and largely symbolic. The monarch's role is primarily ceremonial, representing the unity and continuity of the nation. While the monarchy symbolizes tradition and stability, it also acts as a unifying figure for the diverse peoples of the United Kingdom and the Commonwealth realms, where the Queen is also the head of state.

One of the most crucial aspects of the monarchy is its relationship with the government and the political system. The British monarchy is a constitutional monarchy, which means that it coexists with a parliamentary democracy. The Queen, as the head of state, performs important ceremonial duties such as the state opening of Parliament, the granting of royal assent, and the appointment of the Prime Minister. However, the power to govern lies with the elected officials and the Prime Minister, who is the head of government. The monarchy's involvement in political matters is strictly limited and it is expected to remain neutral and politically impartial.

Despite its limitations, the monarchy continues to hold considerable influence both domestically and internationally. As a symbol of national identity, the Queen represents the British people, their history, and traditions. The monarchy also plays a crucial role in fostering diplomatic relations with other countries. State visits, where the Queen or other members of the royal family receive foreign dignitaries, provide a platform for building relationships and promoting British interests abroad.

Another significant aspect of the monarchy is its economic impact. The monarchy contributes to tourism, attracting millions of visitors each year who are eager to witness the splendor and grandeur associated with British royalty. Whether it is the Changing of the Guard at Buckingham Palace or a glimpse of the Crown Jewels at the Tower of London, the monarchy adds a dash of glamour and allure to the tourism industry, benefiting the economy as a whole.

The monarchy also extends its influence through philanthropic and charitable endeavors. Members of the royal family are involved in a wide range of charitable organizations and causes, aiming to make a positive impact on society. Their patronages and endorsements raise awareness and provide much-needed support for various issues such as healthcare, education, and conservation.

While the monarchy remains a revered institution for many, it is not without its critics. Some argue that the monarchy is an outdated and unnecessary relic of the past, suggesting that a republic or a more streamlined system would better suit modern democratic ideals. Others raise concerns about the cost to the taxpayer, as the monarchy receives public funds to cover official expenses and activities. As a constitutional monarchy, it plays a vital ceremonial role while respecting the powers of the elected representatives. The monarchy's influence extends beyond politics, as it contributes to the economy, represents the country internationally, and supports charitable causes. While debates surrounding its relevance and cost continue, the monarchy remains an integral part of British society, embodying centuries of history and capturing the imagination of people around the world.

Chapter 2: Early British Monarchs

Origins of the British monarchy

To trace the origins of the British monarchy, we must begin by looking into the concept of kingship itself. Throughout history, kingship has been a common form of governance in many societies, often associated with divine or sacred authority. In early civilizations, such as ancient Egypt and Mesopotamia, the king was considered a representative of the gods and was responsible for maintaining order and harmony within the kingdom. These early examples demonstrate the ancient roots of the concept of kingship, which later influenced the development of the British monarchy.

The British monarchy as we know it today can be traced back to the early medieval period. Following the decline of the Roman Empire in the 5th century AD, Britain was divided and ruled by various kingdoms. It was during this time that the Anglo-Saxon kings began to emerge as powerful rulers. The Anglo-Saxon monarchy was initially characterized by a system of tribal chiefdoms, with each kingdom having its own king. However, as these kingdoms started to merge and the territories expanded, a stronger central authority was needed.

The consolidation of the Anglo-Saxon kingdoms into a single monarchy began with the crowning of King Æthelstan in 924 AD. Æthelstan's reign marked the establishment of a united England and the beginning of the English monarchy. From this point onwards, the English monarchy evolved and adapted to the changing political and social landscape of the country.

One of the key developments in the evolution of the British monarchy was the Norman Conquest in 1066. William the Conqueror, Duke of Normandy, successfully invaded England and established Norman rule. This event had a profound impact on the monarchy, as it brought about significant changes in governance and administration. The Normans introduced a centralized system of government, granting the king more power and establishing strong feudal ties between the monarch and the nobility. The Norman period also saw the introduction of the Domesday Book, a comprehensive survey of England's land and resources, which further strengthened royal control.

Over the centuries, the British monarchy continued to evolve and adapt to various challenges and demands. From the Magna Carta in 1215, which limited the king's powers and established the principles of rule of law, to the Wars of the Roses in the 15th century, which saw the rival houses of Lancaster and York competing for the throne, the monarchy faced numerous trials and tribulations. However, it also demonstrated its ability to endure and maintain its position as a symbol of stability and continuity in the face of these challenges.

The Tudor period marked a significant turning point in the history of the British monarchy. The reigns of Henry VIII, Mary I, and Elizabeth I brought about profound religious, political, and social changes. The break with the Catholic Church and the establishment of the Church of England under Henry VIII had far-reaching consequences for the monarchy. It led to increased royal authority and control, as well as religious tensions that would continue to shape the monarchy's role and influence.

The 17th century was a turbulent time for the British monarchy, marked by the English Civil War and the ultimate execution of King Charles I in 1649. The monarchy was temporarily abolished, and England was ruled as a republic, known as the Commonwealth of England. However, the restoration of the monarchy in 1660, under Charles II, brought back stability and set the stage for a new era of the British monarchy.

Since then, the British monarchy has maintained a central role in British society, although its powers have been gradually curtailed over time. The constitutional reforms of the 18th and 19th centuries, including the Bill of Rights in 1689 and the Act of Settlement in 1701, established important principles and limits on the monarchy's authority. These reforms made it clear that the monarch's powers were to be exercised within the framework of a constitutional monarchy, with an elected government and a system of checks and balances.

Today, the British monarchy continues to serve as a symbol of national identity and unity. While it no longer possesses the same level of political power as it once did, the monarchy plays an important ceremonial and symbolic role. The British monarch, currently Queen Elizabeth II, serves as the head of state and performs various duties and responsibilities, such as opening and closing parliamentary sessions and representing the United Kingdom on state visits. From the tribal chiefdoms of the Anglo-Saxon period to the powerful institution it is today, the British monarchy has adapted and endured, shaping and being shaped by British society. Understanding its historical origins is essential for appreciating the role and significance of the British monarchy in modern times.

Alfred the Great and the House of Wessex

This book serves as a comprehensive exploration of Alfred's life, achievements, and the enduring impact of the House of Wessex on the history and development of England. Delving into both historical accounts and contemporary interpretations, we seek to unravel the true essence of this remarkable monarch and shed light on the House of Wessex's profound contributions to the shaping of a nation.

Origins of the House of Wessex:

Before we embark on the tale of Alfred, it is crucial to understand the roots of the House of Wessex. The Wessex dynasty emerged during the early 6th century when the legendary figure of Cerdic, descended from the Saxon migration, established his rule in the region that would later become Wessex. This humble beginning marked the foundation of a lineage that would gradually evolve into a powerhouse of Anglo-Saxon England, culminating in the reign of Alfred the Great.

Alfred's Early Years:

Alfred was born in the year 849 to King Aethelwulf of Wessex and his wife, Osburh. Even from an early age, Alfred exhibited intelligence and an insatiable appetite for learning. As the youngest child of the royal family, he was not expected to ascend to the throne; however, fate had different plans. With the untimely deaths of his older brothers, Alfred unexpectedly became the chosen heir to the throne, thrusting him into a world of political intrigue and warfare at a tender age.

The Dark Days of Viking Invasion:

One cannot speak of Alfred the Great without acknowledging the immense challenges he faced from Viking invasions. During his reign, the Great Heathen Army ravaged the lands of England, pillaging and plundering as they pleased. These brutal raids left the country in a state of constant fear and uncertainty, threatening the very existence of the Anglo-Saxon kingdoms. It was in the face of this formidable enemy that Alfred proved his mettle, showcasing a unique blend of military strategy, diplomacy, and determination.

Alfred the Strategist:

Alfred's brilliance lay not only in his ability to defend against Viking onslaughts but also in his foresight to fortify his kingdom's defenses. He prioritized military reformation, establishing a well-trained and disciplined army that could effectively counter the Viking raiders. Recognizing the importance of naval power, Alfred also initiated the construction of a formidable fleet, ensuring the protection of coastal territories. His strategic mind was not limited to defense, as he also devised plans to retake captured territories and expand his influence.

The Alfredian Renaissance:

Beyond his military endeavors, Alfred the Great was a champion of education and cultural advancement. His reign marked what later came to be known as the "Alfredian Renaissance." Recognizing the dearth of literacy in his kingdom, Alfred made it his mission to promote education among his subjects. He translated numerous works from Latin into Old English, making knowledge accessible to those who had been previously excluded. By fostering a climate of learning and intellectual curiosity, Alfred laid the foundations for the development of a thriving Anglo-Saxon culture.

Legacy of the House of Wessex:

Although Alfred the Great reigned for just under three decades, his impact on England and its subsequent history is immeasurable. The House of Wessex, through Alfred's visionary leadership and subsequent monarchs, established a lineage of rulers who nourished the nation. Their legacy endured beyond Alfred's death, with his descendants continuing his work and guiding England through both turmoil and triumph. The House of Wessex became a symbol of continuity, resilience, and a shared identity for the English people.

In uncovering the remarkable story of Alfred the Great and the House of Wessex, we find ourselves immersed in a tale of strength, determination, and intellectual growth. Alfred's legacy is one of visionary leadership, strategic thinking, and a commitment to the betterment of his people. Through this exploration, we hope to shed light on the extraordinary historical figures who shaped England's destiny and inspire readers to further explore this fascinating era of British history.

William the Conqueror and the Norman influence

As we embark on this journey, it is essential to understand the context in which William the Conqueror emerged as a formidable leader. Born in 1028, he ascended to the dukedom of Normandy at a tender age of seven. His upbringing, surrounded by political intrigue and rivalries, undoubtedly shaped his character and strategies as a ruler. Determined to consolidate his power, William focused on expanding his territories in France, leading to several military campaigns and conflicts. These experiences not only instilled in him a military prowess but also honed his skills as a statesman and administrator.

The pivotal moment in William's life and the highlight of his reign was the invasion of England in 1066. This audacious venture, later known as the Norman Conquest, was sparked by William's claim to the English throne, which he believed was rightfully his. He successfully defeated the English forces led by King Harold II at the Battle of Hastings, forever altering the course of England's history. This singular event marked the beginning of a profound Norman influence on the British Isles.

One of the most significant contributions of the Normans was the sweeping changes they made to the English governance system. William implemented a centralized feudal system, replacing the previous Anglo-Saxon system. This led to the establishment of a powerful Norman nobility and a strong monarchy that asserted its authority over the land. The Normans introduced a rigorous administrative framework that brought stability and efficiency to England's governance, setting the stage for centuries of political development.

Additionally, the Normans played a crucial role in shaping the English legal and judicial systems. William's reign saw the compilation of the Domesday Book, a comprehensive survey of landownership and taxation, which provided valuable insights into England's socioeconomic structure. In a broader sense, this signaled the beginnings of an extensive bureaucratic apparatus that would form the foundation of the modern British legal and economic systems. The Norman influence would further enrich the legal landscape by introducing the concept of "trial by jury," a principle still deeply ingrained in today's legal practices.

The cultural impact of the Normans cannot be overstated. They brought with them a sophisticated and refined way of life, which greatly influenced English society. The Norman ruling class embraced a distinct architectural style, characterized by grand castles, imposing cathedrals, and fortified buildings. These structures, such as the iconic Tower of London, showcased their wealth, power, and artistic sensibilities. The Normans also introduced French as the language of the elite, which became the language of the court and the ruling classes. Although Old English continued to be spoken by the general population, the infusion of French vocabulary into the language enriched and shaped what eventually became Middle English.

Beyond architecture and language, the Normans left an indelible mark on English literature, both religious and secular. Monastic centers, established or reinvigorated under Norman patronage, became centers of learning and intellectual development. Religious texts were translated and preserved, setting the stage for the flourishing of Gothic architecture and the rise of the English Church. Secular literature also thrived during this period, with the famous works of Geoffrey Chaucer and the Arthurian legends reflecting the Norman influence on English storytelling traditions.

As we conclude this exploration of William the Conqueror and the Norman influence, it becomes evident that their impact was far-reaching and profound. From political and administrative reforms to legal and cultural transformations, the Normans exerted a lasting influence on England and beyond. William's audacious conquest and his subsequent reign marked a pivotal moment in history that fundamentally changed the fabric of the British Isles.

Today, we can still see glimpses of the Norman influence in our institutions, language, and cultural practices. It is a testament to the enduring legacy of William the Conqueror and the transformative impact of the Normans. As we dive deeper into the ones of this book, we will unravel the intricacies of their conquest, explore the key figures that shaped this era, and shed light on the lasting implications that continue to illuminate our understanding of history.

Chapter 3: Tudor Dynasty

Henry VIII and the break from the Catholic Church

Known for his larger-than-life personality and infamous marital exploits, Henry VIII's decision to break from the Catholic Church in the 16th century remains one of the most pivotal moments in English history. This essay aims to shed light on the factors that led to this dramatic split and explore its consequences for both the religious and political landscape of the time.

Background:
At the heart of Henry VIII's break from the Catholic Church lies the issue of his quest for a male heir. His first wife, Catherine of Aragon, had failed to bear him a son who survived infancy, leaving the legitimacy of his dynasty in question. When Henry became enamored with Anne Boleyn and desired to marry her, he sought an annulment from the Catholic Church, claiming his marriage to Catherine was invalid due to her previous marriage to his deceased brother. The refusal of Pope Clement VII to grant the annulment prompted Henry VIII to pursue a path that would ultimately unravel centuries of religious tradition and reshape England's ecclesiastical landscape.

Motivations:
While the quest for a male heir played a prominent role in Henry VIII's break from the Catholic Church, it was by no means the sole factor. Henry's newfound infatuation with Anne Boleyn certainly fueled his desire to sever ties with Rome, but underlying this personal motivation were also broader political and ideological drivers. By breaking with Rome, Henry sought to consolidate his power as the Supreme Head of the Church of England, placing himself firmly at the center of both religious and political authority. Additionally, the Reformation sweeping across Europe offered a theological justification for those questioning Catholic doctrines, and Henry seized this opportunity to detach England

from the Pope's control.

Reformation in England:
With the Act of Supremacy in 1534, Henry VIII declared himself as the supreme head of the Church of England, severing all ties to the authority of the Pope in Rome. The dissolution of the monasteries followed, as Henry sought to consolidate and redistribute the immense wealth held by the Roman Catholic Church in England. Monastic institutions were dissolved, their property seized, and religious orders disbanded. This marked a significant shift in religious power and land ownership, as well as a momentous change in the religious practices and rituals of the English people.

Consequences and Legacies:
The break from the Catholic Church and the establishment of the Church of England held profound consequences for England's religious and political landscape. The religious infrastructure was restructured with Henry VIII's ecclesiastical appointments, which sought to ensure loyalty to the crown. The English Reformation also led to a wave of religious reformers and dissenters, such as Thomas Cranmer and Thomas Cromwell, who played significant roles in shaping the theological direction of the emerging Anglican Church.

Furthermore, the break from Rome set England on a separate trajectory from Catholic Europe, impacting its geopolitical positioning and ultimately contributing to a distinct English national identity. This division would continue to reverberate throughout history, with subsequent monarchs and religious leaders influencing the practice and progression of the Anglican Church. The legacy of Henry VIII's split from the Catholic Church would shape not only the religious landscape of England but also its political, social, and cultural developments for centuries to come.

Henry VIII's decision to break from the Catholic Church in the 16th century was a significant turning point in English history, with far-reaching consequences that continue to shape the nation today. Motivated by personal desires, political motivations, and aligned with the broader Protestant Reformation sweeping across Europe, Henry's actions transformed England's religious and political landscape. The establishment of the Church of England and the severing of ties with Rome forged a unique path for England, setting it apart from its Catholic counterparts and laying the groundwork for the development of the Anglican tradition. The ramifications of this break are a testament to the far-reaching power and influence of one monarch's decisions.

Elizabeth I and the Golden Age of England

One of the defining characteristics of Elizabethan England was its cultural vibrancy and creativity. The queen herself was a patron of the arts and possessed a keen interest in literature, drama, and music. The flourishing of literature during this era saw renowned writers like William Shakespeare, Christopher Marlowe, and Edmund Spenser emerge. The works produced during this period helped shape English literature and continue to be studied and celebrated today. Additionally, the growth of the theater industry, exemplified by the construction of the Globe Theatre, allowed for the popularization of plays that entertained and educated both the elite and the commoners. The Elizabethan era was undoubtedly a time of artistic enlightenment, which contributed significantly to the creation of a distinctly English identity.

In addition to its cultural achievements, the Golden Age of England was marked by significant political stability under the rule of Elizabeth I. This era witnessed the establishment of a robust monarchy that effectively balanced power between the crown and Parliament. Elizabeth's decision to maintain a strong central authority while granting some power to Parliament was a delicate political maneuver that prevented the nation from descending into the chaos witnessed in previous reigns. Furthermore, her diplomatic skills and careful management of foreign relations allowed England to establish itself as a dominant player on the international stage. The defeat of the Spanish Armada in 1588 not only secured England's status as a naval power but also solidified Elizabeth's position as a respected leader among European monarchs. The political stability and successes of Elizabeth's reign laid the groundwork for the subsequent growth and expansion of England as a global empire.

Economically, the reign of Elizabeth I witnessed significant advancements that contributed to the prosperity of England. The expansion of overseas trade and exploration during this period allowed for the accumulation of wealth and the establishment of colonies in the New World. The rise of merchant ventures such as the Muscovy Company and the East India Company led to the growth of both domestic and international trade, resulting in increased economic opportunities for the English people. The development of a thriving merchant class, along with advancements in agricultural techniques, contributed to a steady increase in the nation's overall wealth. Furthermore, Elizabeth's policies promoting investment in industries such as textiles and mining helped diversify the economy and stimulate growth. The economic prosperity witnessed during the Golden Age of England not only generated financial stability but also funded the cultural and political developments that defined the era.

It is also important to acknowledge the impact of Elizabeth I's personal attributes and leadership style on the Golden Age of England. Her intelligence, political astuteness, and unwavering determination were instrumental in guiding the nation through a period of immense change and uncertainty. Elizabeth's ability to balance pragmatism and charisma allowed her to command the respect and loyalty of her subjects, even in the face of religious divisions and political rivalries. As a female monarch in a predominantly male-dominated world, Elizabeth faced unique challenges and expectations. However, her shrewd governance and ability to assert authority ensured her longevity on the throne and the stability of the nation. Moreover, Elizabeth's strong sense of national pride and desire to elevate England's standing in the world helped shape the identity of the nation and set the stage for future achievements. The cultural vibrancy, political stability, and economic prosperity witnessed during this era have left an indelible mark on the nation's identity and continue to shape our understanding of England's past. Elizabeth's unwavering leadership, combined with the advancements in literature, theater, trade, and exploration, laid the foundations for modern-day England and allowed the nation to assert itself as a global power. The legacy of Elizabeth I and her Golden Age continues to captivate the imagination and inspire further exploration of this remarkable period in history.

The Stuart succession and the English Civil War

The Stuart succession marked a significant transition in the English monarchy. The reign of Elizabeth I, the last Tudor monarch, concluded in 1603 with her death. As she had no children, the throne passed to her cousin, James VI of Scotland, who became James I of England. This union of the crowns of Scotland and England under a single monarch paved the way for the Stuart dynasty. However, this transition was not without its challenges, as James faced cultural and political differences between Scotland and England.

The religious landscape during the Stuart succession played a crucial role in shaping the events that led to the English Civil War. The Reformation had introduced Protestantism to England, but tensions between different religious denominations persisted. The Stuart monarchs, particularly James I and his son Charles I, sought to impose a more centralized form of Anglicanism, which clashed with the beliefs of Puritans and other dissenting groups. This religious conflict, combined with political tensions, created a volatile atmosphere that culminated in the outbreak of the Civil War.

The English Civil War, which lasted from 1642 to 1651, was a pivotal moment in English history. It was a complex conflict that arose from a confluence of political, religious, and socio-economic factors. On one side stood the Royalists, loyal to the king and the established order, while on the other side were the Parliamentarians, who sought to limit the king's powers and establish a more representative government. These opposing factions clashed in a series of military campaigns that reshaped the political landscape of England and ultimately led to the overthrow and execution of King Charles I.

The causes of the English Civil War were multi-faceted. Political tensions between the monarchy and Parliament had been brewing for years, with the king's attempts to assert his authority conflicting with Parliament's desire to protect the rights and liberties of the people. Economic factors also played a role, as some members of Parliament were concerned with the king's financial management and the burden of taxation. Additionally, the religious divide between Anglicans and dissenting groups like Puritans created deep-seated conflicts that fueled the flames of war.

The course of the English Civil War saw a series of military engagements and political maneuvering. Initially, the Royalists held the upper hand, as Charles I commanded a formidable army and the support of many nobles. However, as the

Parliamentarians organized themselves under leaders such as Oliver Cromwell, the tide began to turn. Cromwell's New Model Army proved to be a disciplined and effective fighting force, ultimately leading to the defeat of the Royalists at the Battle of Naseby in 1645.

The aftermath of the Civil War brought about a period of political instability and experimentation. The execution of Charles I in 1649 marked a radical departure from the traditional notion of kingship and led to the establishment of the Commonwealth, a republican government led by Cromwell. This new era witnessed various political and social transformations, such as religious toleration, military rule, and expansionist policies abroad. However, Cromwell's rule was not without controversy and was met with opposition from Royalists, Levellers, and other groups.

With the Restoration of the monarchy in 1660, under Charles II, England began a process of reconciliation and stability. The Stuart succession was temporarily restored, and efforts were made to heal the wounds caused by the Civil War. However, many of the underlying tensions and divisions remained, setting the stage for future conflicts and shaping the trajectory of English history. By tracing the events and exploring the underlying causes, we hope to shed light on this fascinating period in history. The dynamics of power, religion, and social tensions during this time continue to reverberate through British society, making the study of these topics essential for understanding the development of the nation.

Chapter 4: Hanoverian Kings

George III and the American Revolution

Amidst this backdrop, George III, the reigning monarch of Great Britain during the crucial years leading up to the revolution, played a significant role that has often been oversimplified or misunderstood. By examining the actions, beliefs, and influence of George III, this one aims to shed light on the complex dynamic between the King and the American Revolution, exploring the factors that led to the uprising of the thirteen colonies against British rule.

George III: Ruler and Beliefs:

To comprehensively understand George III's role in the American Revolution, we must begin by delving into his character as a ruler and his personal beliefs. Ascending to the throne in 1760, George III was deeply committed to the idea of monarchy and firmly believed in the divine right of kings. His worldview emphasized the monarch's duty to protect and govern his subjects, a view that would have far-reaching implications as tensions mounted in the American colonies. Despite his earnest intentions, his stubbornness and limited understanding of the colonial populations contributed to the growing discontent that ultimately fueled the revolution.

Taxation, Colonial Resentment, and the King's Response:

A primary point of contention between Britain and the American colonies was the issue of taxation. The King, supported by his advisors, endorsed policies such as the Stamp Act, Townshend Acts, and the Tea Act, which were implemented to alleviate Britain's escalating debt. However, these measures were met with significant resistance from the American colonists, who saw them as blatant infringements on their rights and liberties. Faced with mounting tensions, George III struggled to comprehend the depth of colonial resentment, trusting instead in the advice of his ministers. This disconnection between the monarchy and the colonists only exacerbated the divide, providing fertile ground for revolutionary sentiment to take root.

The Proclamation of 1763 and Its Ramifications:

The Proclamation of 1763, issued by King George III following the French and Indian War, further strained the relationship between Britain and the colonies. The proclamation aimed to prevent conflicts between colonists and Native American tribes by restricting westward expansion beyond the Appalachian Mountains. While George III's intention was to maintain peace, this measure was seen by the colonists as an undue restriction on their growth and expansion. The Proclamation further deepened the colonists' growing sense of alienation and frustration, reinforcing their emerging identity as independent entities separate from the British Crown.

Role of George III in the Execution of British Policy:

As monarch, George III had the power to shape the direction of British policy towards the American colonies. Although Parliament played a vital role in formulating legislation, the King had the authority to veto or endorse bills, granting him significant influence. While it is crucial not to overstate George III's direct control over legislative decisions, his support for measures such as the Coercive Acts and the suppression of dissent in Boston following the Boston Tea Party cemented his association with unpopular policies, further fueling colonial grievances. In this regard, George III found himself leading a kingdom divided, with his inability to effectively manage dissent contributing to the escalation of tensions and ultimately, to the American Revolution.

George III's Legacy:

The American Revolution dealt a severe blow to George III's reign, tarnishing his reputation and casting him as a tyrant in the eyes of many colonists who sought independence. The war's outcome, with Britain ultimately conceding defeat and recognizing the sovereignty of the United States, forever changed the course of history. George III's reign can be seen as a pivotal moment in the relationship between monarchy and subject, as it underscored the importance of listening to and understanding the needs and desires of a diverse population.

Ultimately, it serves as a reminder of the complex interplay between individual rulers, political institutions, and the aspirations of a nation.

George III and the American Revolution cannot be understood in isolation. Through a nuanced examination of the King's beliefs, his role in executing policies, and the colonial response, we gain insight into the multifaceted factors that shaped this critical period in history. While George III is often portrayed as the antagonist of the American Revolution, it is essential to recognize the broader political, social, and ideological tensions that propelled the colonies toward independence. By uncovering the complexities of George III's reign, this one seeks to promote a deeper understanding of the forces that led to the birth of a new nation and the enduring legacy of this remarkable era.

Queen Victoria and the Victorian era

To truly understand Queen Victoria and the Victorian era, it is essential to appreciate the political and economic context of the time. The 19th century was a time of tremendous change, as Britain transitioned from an agrarian society to an industrial powerhouse. Queen Victoria ascended to the throne at the young age of 18, and her reign coincided with the peak of the Industrial Revolution. This era witnessed rapid urbanization, the rise of the working class, and the accompanying social and political challenges that emerged. The Queen's reign also saw Britain experience significant imperial expansion, with the British Empire reaching its zenith. It is within this context that Queen Victoria's leadership and influence must be examined.

Queen Victoria's reign was marked by a unique combination of tradition and progressiveness. On the one hand, she embraced the traditional roles and responsibilities of a monarch, upholding moral values and exemplifying the virtues of the Victorian era. On the other hand, she also played a pivotal role in initiating and supporting social reforms that aimed to address some of the most pressing issues of the time. The Queen's personal life, particularly her marriage to Prince Albert, played a crucial role in shaping her attitudes and actions. Their union was one of deep affection and partnership, and Prince Albert became an influential advisor to the Queen. Together, they championed causes such as education, health reforms, and the abolition of slavery. Queen Victoria's passion for philanthropy and her active involvement in charitable work endeared her to the public and solidified her reputation as the "people's monarch."

The Victorian era was a time of immense cultural and artistic flourishment, characterized by a distinct aesthetic that continues to define our perception of the period. This era witnessed the rise of the middle class, who sought to replicate the opulence and refinement of the aristocracy. The architecture of the time reflected this aspiration, with grand Victorian houses and Gothic revival buildings becoming symbols of wealth and status. Additionally, the Victorian era witnessed significant advancements in the field of literature, with authors such as Charles Dickens, Charlotte Brontë, and Oscar Wilde producing iconic works that continue to be celebrated today. These literary creations captured the essence of Victorian society, highlighting both its virtues and its flaws. Art and design were also flourishing during this period, with the Pre-Raphaelite Brotherhood redefining the artistic landscape through their commitment to nature and meticulous attention to detail.

However, it is important to recognize that the Victorian era was not without its challenges and controversies. As industrialization progressed, the working class faced grueling working conditions and economic inequality, leading to social unrest. The era also witnessed the struggle for women's rights, with notable figures such as suffragette Emmeline Pankhurst fighting for gender equality. Moreover, the widespread influence of imperialism and colonialism during this time had profound consequences for both the British Empire and the countries it subjugated. These dark ones of the Victorian era must also be acknowledged as part of its larger narrative. This period of British history witnessed significant social, political, and cultural changes that continue to shape our world today. Queen Victoria's reign, with its unique blend of tradition and progressiveness, played a pivotal role in propelling these transformations forward. Her influence and the advancements of the era are still palpable in various aspects of contemporary society. By delving into the multifaceted aspects of Queen Victoria and the Victorian era, we can gain a deeper understanding of this transformative period and appreciate its enduring legacy.

George V and the decline of European monarchies

In this regard, the reign of George V, from 1910 to 1936, emerged as a pivotal moment that signified a turning point in the decline of European monarchies. This essay aims to examine George V's rule and its significance in the broader context of European monarchies by exploring the social, political, and cultural forces that shaped this era. By delving into the events and influences that disrupted traditional monarchical power structures, we can better understand the changing role of royalty during this transformative period.

The Context of Decline:
To grasp the significance of George V's reign amidst the decline of European monarchies, it is essential to acknowledge the political and societal backdrop that catalyzed these changes. The early 20th century witnessed a tide of democratic movements sweeping across the continent, fueled by ideals of equality and demands for representative government. The autocratic institutions of monarchy, which had for centuries held considerable authority and influence, suddenly found themselves grappling with wavering support and societal pressure. Alongside this, the catastrophic impact of World War I shattered the illusion of divine right, exposing the limitations and vulnerabilities of monarchical rule. In this atmosphere of shifting paradigms, the figureheads of European monarchies faced unprecedented challenges to their existence and relevance.

George V's Reforms and Adaptation:
Enter George V, regarded as a deeply committed and astute monarch who recognized the need for the British monarchy to evolve with the times. His reign was marked by several bold reforms that aimed to maintain the relevance and stability of the institution amidst mounting pressures. Notably, George V relinquished much of the monarch's personal political power, transferring it to more democratic institutions and emphasizing the ceremonial role of the crown. This gesture not only reflected a willingness to adapt to changing societal expectations but also showcased the versatility and resilience of the monarchy in a rapidly evolving world. George V leveraged his position to rebuild public trust in the monarchy and redefine its purpose within a democratic framework.

The British Commonwealth Connection:
One factor that greatly contributed to the resilience of the British monarchy during this era was its association with the Commonwealth. Established during George V's reign, the Commonwealth marked a shift from a colonial relationship to a cooperative and voluntary association of nations. By transforming colonial dependencies into equal partners and emphasizing shared values, the British monarchy managed to navigate the changing political landscape without surrendering its symbolic and diplomatic influence. Through the Commonwealth, George V successfully maintained ties to former colonies, promoting cultural exchange and diplomatic cooperation, ensuring the continued relevance of the monarchy even in a post-imperial world.

Myth vs. Reality: The Impact of World War I:
The first World War had a profound impact on the stability and perception of European monarchies, shaking their legitimacy and eroding the notion of divine right. Soldiers returning from the horrors of the war questioned the very foundations of monarchy, having witnessed the ultimate sacrifice of their fellow comrades. The fall of several monarchies in Europe, such as the collapse of the German Empire and the Austro-Hungarian Empire, highlighted the vulnerability of these institutions. However, George V managed to navigate this turbulent period through careful diplomacy, adopting a humane and approachable style that endeared him to the British people. By balancing tradition and empathy, George V reinforced the monarchy's role as a symbol of stability and unity in the aftermath of the Great War.

The Rise of Republicanism and Class Struggles:
Beyond the impact of war, the early 20th century was marked by a growing tide of republican sentiment and an increasing focus on social justice and equality. These shifts in societal values escalated class struggles and fostered a broader rejection of traditional aristocracy. It is in this context that George V's reign stands out, as he managed to maintain the monarchy's popularity and adapt to the changing times. By projecting an image of relatability and compassion, George V won over the hearts and minds of the British people, presenting himself as a unifying figurehead rather than a privileged aristocrat. This approach helped neutralize republican sentiment and sustain the monarchy amidst an evolving social fabric.

The reign of George V occupies a significant place in European history, encapsulating the profound changes and challenges experienced by monarchies in the early 20th century. Through his reforms, adaptability, and astute diplomacy, George V succeeded in navigating the decline of European monarchies, ensuring the survival and transformation of the British monarchy. His reign not only reduced the concentration of royal power but also positioned the monarchy as a symbol of stability, unity, and resilience in an ever-changing world. By studying George V's reign, we can shed light on the broader dynamics that contributed to the decline of European monarchies, while also appreciating the adaptability and relevance of this enduring institution.

Chapter 5: Windsors through the 20th Century

King Edward VIII and the abdication crisis

The abdication crisis of King Edward VIII merits our attention due to the intricate blend of personal sentiment and royal duty that enveloped this significant event. Let us begin with the background, shall we. Edward VIII ascended to the throne in January 1936, following the death of his father, King George V. Though initially displaying an affable and charismatic disposition, his reign soon became overshadowed by his relationship with Wallis Simpson, a divorced American woman. This liaison, which was viewed as scandalous and utterly unsuitable for a king, created a divisive divide within the British establishment. It raised concerns of political instability and, further still, brought into question the role of the monarchy in modern societal norms.

The abdication crisis reached its pinnacle towards the end of 1936, as King Edward VIII's love for Wallis Simpson began to collide with his responsibilities as a constitutional monarch. Prime Minister Stanley Baldwin, upon acknowledging the detrimental effects of the relationship on the monarchy and politics, made it clear that the British government would find it difficult to support a marriage between the king and Simpson. Faced with an ultimatum, King Edward VIII made the astonishing decision that stunned the nation and the world: he chose love over his position as king. On December 10, 1936, he made a heartfelt and historic radio broadcast, indicating his intention to abdicate the throne, simultaneously expressing his desire to marry Simpson and his inability to fulfill his royal duties without her as his consort.

This radical decision was met with a maelstrom of reactions, both positive and negative, from different sectors of society. The Edwardians, those committed supporters of the king, felt a sense of betrayal, appalled by the thought that the king chose personal happiness over the duties and responsibilities inherent in his role. However, the broader public, particularly in America, found themselves captivated by the story, perceiving the king's abdication as an act of romantic heroism. The press played a significant role in shaping public opinion, often focusing on the king's undying love for Wallis Simpson. It is worth noting that the abdication crisis occurred during a time of economic hardship and political uncertainty, both domestically and internationally. This context further contributed to the public's fascination with the personal lives of their monarchs, as it offered an escape from the harsh realities of the world.

The abdication crisis had profound implications for the British monarchy itself, as it exposed inherent weaknesses within the institution. The crisis highlighted the strains placed on the monarchy when confronted with personal choices that clashed with public expectations and political realities. Consequently, it led to a gradual shift towards an institution that must be more accountable to public opinion and contemporary societal standards. The crisis also sparked debates regarding the role of marriage within the monarchy, as the church and society held steadfast beliefs regarding the sanctity of marriage, particularly when it came to marrying divorcees.

Internationally, the abdication crisis had far-reaching consequences, affecting British relationships with other countries and monarchies. European monarchies, who were already facing their own challenges, closely observed the events in Britain, perceiving the abdication as reflective of the changing dynamics within traditional monarchies. It marked a shift towards a more democratic and egalitarian society, where personal feelings and desires seemed to guide the actions of the head of state. This effectively accelerated the transformation of monarchies across Europe, particularly in relation to their roles and powers. Through understanding the circumstances leading up to the crisis, the public reactions, and the lasting impacts it had on the British monarchy and international relations, we gain insight into the complex intersection of personal choices, duties, and societal expectations. The abdication crisis of King Edward VIII represents a significant turning point in British history, forever changing the monarchy and the perceptions surrounding it. It remains a topic of great fascination, never failing to spark heated discussions and continued research, as we seek to comprehend the implications of love and duty on the world stage.

Queen Elizabeth II and her reign as the longest-serving monarch

One of the defining aspects of Queen Elizabeth II's reign is her steadfast commitment to her role as a constitutional monarch. Throughout her time on the throne, she has demonstrated an unwavering dedication to serving her country and its people. Despite holding a largely ceremonial position, the Queen has fulfilled her responsibilities with a deep sense of duty, always putting the interests of her nation first. Whether it be through her public engagements, state visits, or encounters with individuals from all walks of life, Queen Elizabeth II has shown a genuine interest and concern for the well-being of her constituents, fostering a sense of unity and respect among the British people.

In addition to her role as a head of state, Queen Elizabeth II has navigated the complexities of the ever-evolving modern world, adapting to societal changes and embracing technological advancements. Through her yearly Christmas broadcasts, the Queen has used television as a platform to address the nation, delivering messages of hope, resilience, and unity. This ability to connect with the British public, regardless of their age or background, has been a testament to her ability to adapt to contemporary forms of communication and maintain relevance in an ever-changing world.

Furthermore, Queen Elizabeth II has overseen significant transformations within the monarchy itself. Her reign has witnessed a change in public perception, particularly through her response to tragedies and national crises. Following the untimely death of Princess Diana in 1997, the Queen faced criticism for her initial handling of the situation but ultimately demonstrated great sensitivity and empathy towards the nation's grief. Her subsequent tribute and acknowledgment of public sentiment allowed her to reclaim the public's affection and solidify her own position as a beloved figurehead.

Moreover, the Queen's reign has coincided with profound political change, including the devolution of power and the decline of the British Empire. She has deftly traversed the shifting political landscape, continuously adapting her role to meet the demands of a modernized United Kingdom. Her efforts to maintain the unity of the Commonwealth and foster relationships with leaders across the globe have contributed to her standing as a respected figure on the international stage. Additionally, Queen Elizabeth II has played a vital role in promoting diplomacy and fostering positive international relations, using state visits as opportunities to strengthen ties with countries far and wide.

The longevity of her reign has allowed Queen Elizabeth II to witness and adapt to numerous changes, while also serving as a bridge between past and present. Through her dedication to charitable causes, the preservation of cultural heritage, and her commitment to public service, the Queen has become a unifying figure within the nation. Her work in supporting various charitable organizations has had a positive and lasting impact on countless individuals and communities throughout the United Kingdom and beyond.

As the longest-serving monarch in British history, Queen Elizabeth II has had an immeasurable impact on her nation and the world at large. Her reign has been characterized by stability, adaptability, and a profound sense of duty. By embracing change while upholding tradition, she has earned the respect and affection of her people and has solidified the monarchy's place in the modern world. Her dedication to her role as a constitutional monarch, her adaptability to modernity, and her ability to navigate challenges with grace and sensitivity have made her an exceptional leader. Throughout her reign, Queen Elizabeth II has consistently placed the interests of her nation and its people at the forefront, embodying the values of duty and service. As we look back at her reign, we cannot help but recognize and appreciate the profound impact she has had on the United Kingdom, the Commonwealth, and the world beyond.

Prince Charles and the modern challenges of the Royal Family

Throughout its long and storied history, the monarchy has faced numerous challenges and has had to adapt to changing times. In recent years, Prince Charles, the eldest son of Queen Elizabeth II, has played a pivotal role in guiding the Royal Family through the complexities of the modern era. This essay will explore the various challenges faced by Prince Charles and the strategies he has employed to address them, highlighting his efforts to modernize and sustain the relevance of the Royal Family in a rapidly changing world.

Challenge 1: Public Perception and Personal Reputation:

One of the key challenges facing Prince Charles has been to shape public perception and manage his personal reputation. Being in the public eye his entire life, Prince Charles has endured a fair share of controversies and scrutiny. His marriage to Princess Diana and the subsequent revelations about their troubled relationship brought a wave of negative press attention. However, instead of shying away from controversy, Prince Charles has taken a proactive stance in addressing public concerns. He has engaged in numerous charitable initiatives, championing causes such as environmental preservation, architecture, and sustainable farming. By showcasing his interests and passions, Prince Charles has been successful in redefining his public image and establishing himself as a dedicated and caring individual.

Challenge 2: Maintaining Relevance in a Changing Society

Another significant challenge faced by the Royal Family has been to maintain relevance amidst the changing societal landscapes. The British monarchy has a long-standing tradition, but with the advent of the digital age and increased scrutiny, the institution has had to evolve to remain appealing to the public. Prince Charles recognized the need to adapt and has embraced technology and social media to engage with a younger audience. For instance, he actively maintains a presence on various social media platforms, sharing updates about his projects and engaging in conversations with his followers. By doing so, Prince Charles has successfully managed to connect with a wider audience, especially among the younger generation, ensuring the longevity and relevance of the institution he represents.

Challenge 3: Succession Planning and the Future of the Monarchy

As the heir apparent to the British throne, Prince Charles has the responsibility of ensuring a seamless transition and succession plan for the monarchy. This challenge has been particularly pronounced due to the increased interest in the personal lives of the Royal Family and the changing attitudes towards the role of the monarchy itself. Prince Charles has taken an active role in preparing his sons, Princes William and Harry, for their future roles as well as involving them in royal duties from an early age. Moreover, Prince Charles has consistently emphasized the importance of the Commonwealth, an association of 54 member countries, as a means of future collaboration and connection. By fostering partnerships and diplomatic relationships, he is not only ensuring the relevance of the monarchy but also paving the way for a smooth transition to the next generation.

Prince Charles has faced a multitude of challenges in his role as a key figure within the Royal Family. However, through his proactive approach, adaptability, and genuine care for important issues, he has successfully navigated these challenges. By addressing public perception, embracing modernization, and preparing for the future, Prince Charles has played a vital role in modernizing and sustaining the relevance of the Royal Family. In doing so, he has secured the institution's place in a rapidly changing world, ensuring its continued significance for years to come.

Chapter 6: Current Generation

Prince William and Kate Middleton

To truly understand their significance, it is essential to explore the individual histories of both Prince William and Kate Middleton. Prince William, born on June 21, 1982, is the eldest son of the late Princess Diana and Prince Charles, the heir to the British throne. Growing up in the spotlight, William faced immense scrutiny and attention from a young age. Despite this, he displayed remarkable resilience and maintained a sense of normalcy, attending school with his peers and participating in extracurricular activities. These formative years undoubtedly shaped him into the compassionate and grounded individual he is today.

Kate Middleton, born on January 9, 1982, had a decidedly different upbringing. She grew up in Bucklebury, Berkshire, the daughter of self-made millionaire parents, Michael and Carole Middleton. Kate attended boarding school before pursuing a degree in Art History at the University of St. Andrews in Scotland, where she would eventually meet her future husband. Kate's down-to-earth personality and strong family values have greatly endeared her to the public, who admire her relatability and genuine nature.

It was during their time at the University of St. Andrews that Prince William and Kate Middleton first crossed paths. Both studying Art History, their shared academic pursuits laid the foundation for a deep connection and blossoming romance. However, it was not until their second year that their relationship turned romantic, and they embarked on a journey that would captivate the world.

Their courtship, like any other, had its fair share of challenges. The constant media attention and scrutiny placed strains on their relationship, and in 2007, they briefly broke up. This period of separation allowed both individuals to focus on their personal growth and priorities. It was a pivotal moment for Prince William and Kate, as they individually realized the depth of their love for one another.

Eventually, fate intervened, and the couple reconciled. In 2010, Prince William proposed to Kate Middleton during a romantic trip to Kenya with a stunning sapphire and diamond engagement ring that had once belonged to his late mother, Princess Diana. The announcement of their engagement brought immense joy and excitement not only to the royal family but also to the global community eager to witness this modern-day fairytale unfold.

On April 29, 2011, Prince William and Kate Middleton tied the knot at Westminster Abbey in a grand ceremony that was watched by millions worldwide. The wedding was marked by moments of genuine emotion and immense pride, as the couple committed themselves to a life of service and dedication to their country. This union represented a new one in the British monarchy, marrying tradition with the modern values and aspirations of the younger generation.

Since their marriage, Prince William and Kate Middleton have gone on to become proud parents of three children: Prince George, Princess Charlotte, and Prince Louis. As parents, they have taken a compassionate and hands-on approach, ensuring that their children grow up with as normal an upbringing as possible while still fulfilling their royal duties. The couple's commitment to family values and their dedication to their children's well-being is evident in their public interactions and the careful protection of their privacy.

Prince William and Kate Middleton have also made significant contributions to a range of charitable causes, leveraging their position and platform to make a positive impact. The Duchess of Cambridge has shown particular interest in early childhood development and mental health, advocating for increased awareness and support. The Duke of Cambridge, on the other hand, has focused on various causes, including environmental conservation and supporting veterans and their families. Through their charitable work, they have acted as beacons of hope and agents of change, inspiring individuals around the world to get involved and make a difference. Through their individual journeys and their shared experiences, they have shown us that despite the weight of their titles and responsibilities, they are relatable and genuine individuals who strive to improve the lives of others. Their story reminds us of the power of love, determination, and compassion, touching the lives of millions and leaving an indelible mark on history.

Prince Harry and Meghan Markle

It represents tradition, heritage, and an embodiment of a nation's identity. But as times change and societies evolve, so too must the monarchy adapt to remain relevant and connect with the public it serves. Prince Harry and Meghan Markle, in their unique position as a modern royal couple, have brought unprecedented changes to the way we perceive and interact with the British monarchy. This book aims to delve into the impact and challenges faced by Prince Harry and Meghan Markle, shedding light on how they have reshaped both the monarchy and wider society.

A Royal Love Story

The story of Prince Harry and Meghan Markle is synonymous with a modern fairytale. Two individuals from different backgrounds and with their own accomplishments found love amidst societal expectations and media scrutiny. Their relationship symbolizes a new era for the monarchy, as Meghan Markle became the first biracial woman to marry into the British royal family. Their union not only showcased the changing dynamics of relationships and who can be considered a suitable partner for a royal, but it also resonated with people worldwide, fostering a sense of inclusivity and diversity.

A Shift in Public Perception

The entrance of Meghan Markle into the royal family brought about a significant shift in public perception. Her background as an actress, activist, and philanthropist led to a fresh and relatable image, attracting attention and admiration from a wider audience. The couple's relatability and transparency in addressing mental health struggles, such as Prince Harry's own experiences, have sparked conversations on a global scale. By bravely discussing their personal battles, they have ignited a movement that destigmatizes mental health issues and encourages open dialogue, revolutionizing the way we approach this sensitive topic.

Challenging Tradition

Prince Harry and Meghan Markle have defied convention and embraced a more progressive approach to their royal roles. Their decision to step back as senior royals and forge their own path, popularly known as "Megxit," was met with both support and criticism. This one explores the motivations behind their move and the subsequent repercussions on the monarchy and public perception. Their desire for a more independent and private life has sparked discussions on the limitations of being born into a royal family and pushed the boundaries of what is traditionally expected in terms of duty and responsibility.

Philanthropy and Activism

Prince Harry and Meghan Markle have spearheaded various philanthropic initiatives and advocacy work. Their shared passion for humanitarian causes has allowed them to draw attention to topics such as gender equality, climate change, mental health awareness, and social justice. This one examines the impact of their activism, their charities, and the pathways they have created for positive change. By utilizing their platform, they have managed to bridge the gap between the royal family and societal issues, challenging the notion that the monarchy is disconnected from the struggles of ordinary people.

Challenges of Media Intrusion

The media's role in shaping public opinion is undeniable, and Prince Harry and Meghan Markle have faced intense scrutiny from the press throughout their relationship. This one delves into the challenges they have encountered with intrusive reporting, the impact it has had on their mental health, and the broader discussion on media ethics and responsibility. The couple's legal battles against tabloids and their decision to limit media access have sparked debates about privacy in the digital age, press freedom, and the all-encompassing nature of fame.

Prince Harry and Meghan Markle's impact on the monarchy and society at large cannot be overstated. Their journey has reshaped the traditional view of the royal family, bringing a renewed sense of inclusivity, relatability, and openness. By challenging conventions, advocating for important causes, and addressing their own struggles, they have redefined what it means to be a modern royal couple. While their choices have faced criticism, they have undeniably sparked crucial conversations and ignited change within the monarchy. Prince Harry and Meghan Markle's unique story continues to captivate the world, showcasing the evolving nature of the monarchy and its intersection with societal transformations.

The future of the British monarchy

One of the key factors that will influence the future of the British monarchy is the changing demographics and attitudes within the United Kingdom. The monarchy has long been a symbol of unity and stability, connecting people from different backgrounds and fostering a sense of shared identity. However, as society becomes more diverse and multicultural, there is a need for the monarchy to adapt and reflect the changing face of the nation. This includes recognizing and celebrating different cultures and traditions, as well as ensuring representation and inclusivity within the royal family. By embracing diversity and actively engaging with various communities, the monarchy can strengthen its relevance and appeal to a wider range of people, ensuring its continued support in the years to come.

Another crucial factor to consider is the role of technology and the media in shaping public perception and expectations of the monarchy. In today's digital age, news travels at lightning speed, and public figures are constantly subjected to scrutiny and analysis. The royal family is no exception to this phenomenon, and their actions and decisions are instantly broadcasted and dissected by the media. This presents both opportunities and challenges for the future of the monarchy. On one hand, technology allows the royal family to directly connect with the public, engaging with them through social media platforms and sharing updates in real-time. This direct interaction can help foster a sense of familiarity and accessibility, breaking down barriers and misconceptions. On the other hand, the constant media attention can also be overwhelming and invasive, impinging on the privacy of the royal family. Striking a balance between maintaining traditional boundaries and embracing modern communication tools will be a delicate task for the monarchy in the future.

Furthermore, the future of the monarchy will be intertwined with the broader political landscape of the United Kingdom. As a constitutional monarchy, the royal family's role is largely ceremonial, representing a sense of continuity and stability in times of political change. Historically, the monarchy has managed to navigate political transitions, adapting to different governments and ideologies while maintaining its influence and relevance. However, as the world becomes increasingly partisan and polarized, it may become more challenging for the monarchy to remain neutral and above the political fray. Balancing their role as constitutional figures with the demands of a changing political climate will require skilled diplomacy and careful navigation. Ensuring that the monarchy remains a unifying force, rather than a divisive one, will be crucial for its continued success and acceptance.

In addition to these internal factors, the future of the British monarchy will also be influenced by external forces and global trends. The monarchy has long had a prominent place on the world stage, with members of the royal family serving as ambassadors and representatives for the United Kingdom. As the world becomes increasingly interconnected and globalized, the monarchy's international role will continue to evolve and expand. This includes not only diplomatic duties but also promoting British businesses, culture, and charitable initiatives on a worldwide scale. By leveraging their unique platform and global appeal, the royal family can play a significant role in promoting British interests and values across the globe. However, this also means that they will face increased scrutiny and expectations from the international community, necessitating adaptability and openness to different cultures and perspectives.

Ultimately, the future of the British monarchy is an inherently uncertain and ever-evolving topic. Predicting the precise course of events is impossible, as it is shaped by numerous interconnected factors and influences. However, what is clear is that the monarchy's long-term survival and success will depend on its ability to adapt and remain relevant in a rapidly changing world. By embracing diversity, engaging with technology, maintaining political neutrality, and expanding their international presence, the royal family can ensure that they continue to hold a meaningful place in the hearts and minds of the British people and the global community. It is through a careful balance of tradition and innovation that the monarchy can secure its future and continue to be a symbol of continuity and unity for generations to come.

Chapter 7: Royal Family Tree

An in-depth look at the genealogy and lineage of British monarchs

To truly appreciate the genealogy of British monarchs, it is essential to begin unraveling these ancestral threads in early history. The roots of the British monarchy can be traced back to the Anglo-Saxon era, with figures like Alfred the Great and Æthelstan playing crucial roles. However, it was not until the Norman Conquest in 1066 that the monarchy as we know it, with its direct lineage, truly began. William the Conqueror's ascent to the throne marked the initiation of a dynasty that still exists today.

From the Norman period onwards, tracing the genealogy of British monarchs becomes a captivating interplay of marriage alliances, political strategies, and dynastic ambitions. For instance, the Plantagenet dynasty, which ruled from the 12th to the 15th centuries, established itself through Henry II's marriage to Eleanor of Aquitaine, thus acquiring vast territories in modern-day France. This dynasty witnessed both the height of England's medieval power and the turmoil of civil wars within the royal family, such as the Wars of the Roses.

The Tudor period, spanning from 1485 to 1603, offers a particularly engaging one in British royal genealogy. Henry VII's victory at the Battle of Bosworth and his subsequent marriage to Elizabeth of York united two warring factions, the Lancastrians and the Yorkists. Their union paved the way for the Tudor dynasty and brought an end to the Wars of the Roses. The reigns of Henry VIII and his children, Edward VI, Mary I, and Elizabeth I, are characterized by religious upheavals, political intrigue, and the bold assertion of royal power.

The Stuart era, which began in 1603 with the accession of James I, introduces us to the intricate connections that linked the British monarchy to continental Europe. James I and his descendants, including Charles I and Charles II, were part of the Stuart dynasty, which originated in Scotland. The marriage between James VI of Scotland and Anne of Denmark further solidified the dynasty's status. However, the Stuart dynasty faced significant challenges, including the English Civil War and the eventual Glorious Revolution, which brought William of Orange and Mary II to power in 1688.

The Hanoverian dynasty, starting with George I in 1714, represented a milestone in British genealogical history. With the Act of Settlement in 1701, which excluded Roman Catholics from the line of succession, the Crown passed to a German-speaking prince from the House of Hanover. George III, who ruled during the American Revolution and the Napoleonic Wars, witnessed significant transformations in political and cultural spheres, reflecting the Enlightenment period's ideals.

The Victorian era, spanning from 1837 to 1901, saw the longest reign in British history under Queen Victoria. Her marriage to Prince Albert of Saxe-Coburg and Gotha exemplified the intertwining of European monarchies. The expansion of the British Empire, the Industrial Revolution's impact, and societal changes shaped this era, leading to the development of constitutional monarchy. Queen Victoria's descendants, including Edward VII, George V, Edward VIII, and George VI, later faced the challenges of the two World Wars.

Today, the British monarchy's genealogy and lineage continue to capture the imagination of people around the world. With Queen Elizabeth II serving as the current monarch, her reign has seen significant milestones, such as her marriage to Prince Philip, the birth of her four children, including Charles, Prince of Wales, and the subsequent generation that includes Prince William, Duke of Cambridge. The monarchy's enduring popularity, despite the evolution of democratic governance, reflects its ability to adapt and maintain a sense of tradition while engaging with contemporary society. From the Norman Conquest to the present day, tracing the familial connections and dynastic alliances enables us to understand the monarchy's development and the individuals who have played pivotal roles along the way. The captivating stories of love, power, and duty that emerge from this genealogy invite us to delve deeper into British royal history, appreciating both the rich tapestry of the monarchy's past and its ongoing relevance in the present day.

Connections to other royal families in Europe

The connections between European royal families can be traced back to ancient times. One of the earliest examples of intermarriage was the union of Princess Theodora, a Byzantine royal, and the Frankish king, Clovis I, in the 6th century. This union not only solidified an alliance between the Frankish and Byzantine empires but also marked the beginning of a tradition that would endure for centuries to come. The strategic nature of these marriages was evident even in this early period, as they aimed to secure alliances, increase national influence, and strengthen political legitimacy.

As the centuries passed, this tradition of intermarriage became even more widespread and complex. The Habsburg dynasty, for instance, built an extensive network of connections through intermarriage that extended far beyond their original realm in Austria. Their marriages with other ruling families such as the Bourbons of France, the Tudors of England, and the Medicis of Italy not only solidified their power but also created a complex web of alliances that could be both beneficial and challenging to navigate.

Another notable example of interconnected royal families is seen in the House of Hanover, whose rulers held both the British and Hanoverian thrones during the 18th century. Through strategic marriages, the Hanoverian monarchs established alliances with other European powers, such as the House of Brandenburg-Prussia and the Romanovs of Russia. These alliances were often forged with the aim of maintaining a balance of power and countering threats from rival states.

The connections between European royal families were not limited to marriages alone. Political alliances and personal friendships also played a significant role in shaping these relationships. For example, the alliance formed between Queen Victoria of England and Prince Albert, her German-born husband, with their extended family across various European royalty, helped shape a sense of European unity amid growing nationalism. The exchange of letters, visits, and personal connections fostered a sense of camaraderie and cooperation among these ruling families, facilitating diplomatic negotiations and strengthening ties between their respective nations.

However, the connections between royal families were not always harmonious. Rivalries, power struggles, and conflicting interests sometimes strained these relationships. The intricate web of alliances, often forged through marriage, had the potential to blur loyalties and fuel conflicts between nations. The 18th and 19th centuries, in particular, witnessed numerous dynastic wars and political upheavals that were driven, at least in part, by the intertwined relationships between European royal families.

The aftermath of World War I marked a significant shift in the dynamics of European monarchy. The rise of republics in several European nations and the fall of autocratic regimes had a profound impact on the interconnectedness of royal families. Many royal houses were abolished, exiled, or reduced to figureheads, leading to a decrease in the influence of monarchies. The marriage alliances between royal families also lost their political significance in this changing landscape, although they continued to be significant in cementing personal and cultural ties.

In the present-day, the connections between European royal families remain characterized by a sense of kinship, tradition, and shared history. While monarchies may no longer wield political power, they continue to serve as cultural symbols and represent the continuity of national heritage. The close relationships between royal families, nurtured through generations of diplomacy and personal connections, continue to be celebrated through state visits, family gatherings, and ceremonial occasions. These relationships, established through intermarriage, political alliances, and personal friendships, have shaped the geopolitical landscape of the continent. While the political influence of monarchies has diminished in modern times, royal families continue to maintain close connections, contributing to a sense of shared heritage and cultural unity. Understanding these connections is essential for comprehending the complex history of Europe's ruling houses and their enduring influence.

Tracing the line of succession

Before we embark on tracing the line of succession, we must first comprehend the importance of this process. In any organization, whether it be a royal family or a corporate entity, a clear succession plan is crucial for ensuring a seamless transfer of responsibilities. The line of succession determines who will assume leadership positions, preventing confusion and conflict that would arise if there were ambiguity surrounding the transfer of power. It allows for the development and grooming of future leaders, ensuring a smooth transition and the preservation of an institution's values and traditions.

To understand the intricacies of tracing the line of succession, it is imperative to examine its historical significance. Throughout history, societies have adopted various methods to determine who would inherit power. The concept of hereditary succession, passing power from one generation to the next within a family, is one of the oldest and most common methods. Many monarchies, for instance, established a clear order of succession based on primogeniture, where the eldest male heir would inherit the throne. This system aimed to maintain stability, avoiding power struggles and potential conflicts.

However, not all societies followed hereditary succession. Some cultures preferred alternative methods, such as elective succession or merit-based systems. For instance, the Holy Roman Empire employed an intricate system known as elective monarchy, where a group of nobles would elect the next ruler. This method aimed to ensure that the most competent and capable candidate took the throne. Similarly, in ancient Rome, the Emperor often appointed his successor based on merit and capabilities, rather than the notion of bloodline inheritance. These alternative succession methods were often utilized to avoid any potential weaknesses that could arise from hereditary succession.

Though tracing the line of succession might seem straightforward, it is often marked by challenges and complexities. One significant challenge lies in determining the criteria for succession. The method chosen must strike a balance between maintaining stability and promoting meritocracy. The use of primogeniture, for instance, may lead to a succession of rulers who lack the necessary skills or qualities needed to govern effectively. On the other hand, systems like elective monarchy can be subject to manipulation and political scheming, resulting in an unstable transition of power. Striking the right balance is key to ensure that the best-suited individual assumes leadership positions.

Furthermore, tracing the line of succession can be impacted by unforeseen circumstances. Unexpected events such as the death of a ruler or the removal of an heir from the line of succession may disrupt the established order. In such cases, determining the next in line becomes a challenging task, often leading to debates and disputes. Rival factions can emerge, each claiming the right to the throne based on their interpretation of the succession law or tradition. In some instances, these disputes have even resulted in civil wars, upending societies and causing significant turmoil. Whether it is within a royal family or any other organization, a clear and well-defined succession plan ensures stability, continuity, and growth. This one has explored the historical significance of tracing the line of succession, the different methods employed throughout time, and the challenges faced in maintaining a seamless transition of power. By understanding the complexities of succession, we can appreciate its importance and navigate the intricacies involved in ensuring a prosperous and sustainable future.

Chapter 8: Royal Scandals and Controversies

Infamous incidents in the history of the British monarchy

It has often been a symbol of stability and continuity, embodying the values and traditions of a nation. However, like any institution, the British monarchy is not immune to controversy and infamy. In this one, we will explore some of the most notorious incidents in the history of the British monarchy. By examining these incidents, we are provided with a deeper understanding of the evolving relationship between the monarchy and the people it governs.

The Execution of King Charles I:

One of the most infamous incidents in British monarchy history occurred in the 17th century with the execution of King Charles I. This event marked the first time a reigning monarch of England, Scotland, and Ireland was put on trial and subsequently executed. The circumstances leading to the execution were complex, with a power struggle between the monarchy and Parliament, fueled by religious and political tensions. Charles I's contentious reign had alienated many parliamentarians, ultimately leading to the English Civil War. The king's trial and subsequent execution shocked Europe and cemented a new era in British history, marked by the rise of Oliver Cromwell's Commonwealth.

Abdication Crisis of 1936:

The Abdication Crisis of 1936 is another well-known incident that occurred within the British monarchy. King Edward VIII's decision to marry an American divorcée, Wallis Simpson, shook the foundations of the institution. At the time, divorce was highly stigmatized, and it was deemed unacceptable for a king to marry a divorcée. Edward VIII was faced with a choice between love and duty, and ultimately abdicated the throne after only 11 months of reign. His brother, King George VI, ascended to the throne, bringing with him a change in the course of history. The Abdication Crisis highlighted the changing social landscape in Britain and the shifting values of the monarchy.

Princess Diana's Death:

In 1997, the tragic death of Princess Diana sent shockwaves across the world, leaving an indelible mark on the British monarchy. Diana, Princess of Wales, had become a beloved figure, known for her tireless charity work and compassion. Her untimely death in a car crash in Paris was met with an outpouring of grief and criticism of the royal family for their perceived lack of empathy and support. The incident led to a profound shift in public perception, pushing the monarchy toward a more approachable and compassionate image. It prompted a reflection on their relationship with the public and their responsibility to show empathy in times of crisis.

Prince Harry and Meghan Markle's 'Megxit':

More recently, the decision by Prince Harry and Meghan Markle to step back as senior members of the royal family, dubbed 'Megxit,' sparked intense media scrutiny and public debate. The couple's desire for a more private life away from constant media attention raised questions about the constraints of royal life and the pressures faced by those within the monarchy. It also exposed underlying issues of racial and societal prejudice within British society. Although the full ramifications of 'Megxit' are yet to be fully understood, it has undoubtedly challenged the traditional perceptions of the monarchy and triggered a reevaluation of its role in the modern world.

Through the exploration of these infamous incidents in the history of the British monarchy, we gain insight into the complex nature of the institution and its evolving relationship with the British people. From the execution of King Charles I and the Abdication Crisis of 1936 to Princess Diana's death and 'Megxit,' each incident has left an indelible mark on the monarchy, shaping its image and influence. By understanding these incidents, we can better appreciate the challenges and triumphs that have shaped the British monarchy and its enduring place in history.

The impact of scandals on the reputation of the Royal Family

Through the years, the Royal Family has faced numerous scandals that have tested their image and influence. These scandals, while diverse in nature, have undeniably affected the reputation of the Royal Family. This essay will delve into the impact of scandals on the Royal Family's reputation and explore how such events have shaped public perceptions over time.

The Historical Context:
To fully comprehend the impact of scandals on the Royal Family's reputation, it is crucial to understand their historical context. The monarchy, as an institution, has evolved significantly over centuries. The Royal Family's reputation used to hinge heavily on notions of divine right and unquestioned authority. However, with the advent of modern media and the increasing scrutiny of public opinion, scandals have become a prominent force in shaping public perception of the monarchy. Today, the Royal Family's reputation relies on their ability to balance tradition and adaptability while avoiding scandals that could potentially damage their standing.

Types of Scandals and their Effects:
Scandals involving the Royal Family can take many forms, ranging from personal relationships to financial improprieties. The effects of these scandals are multifaceted and can impact both individual members and the collective reputation of the monarchy as a whole. Personal scandals, such as extramarital affairs or controversial relationships, attract significant media attention and can severely damage the image of the Royal Family. The fallout from such scandals affects public opinion, potentially eroding the trust and support previously enjoyed.

Financial improprieties, on the other hand, have the potential to tarnish the Royal Family's reputation in terms of ethical conduct and the appropriate use of public funds. These scandals become a matter of public scrutiny, as taxpayers expect the monarchy to be fiscally responsible and transparent with their finances. Failure to meet these expectations can lead to a loss of public trust and perpetuate negative perceptions of the Royal Family, resulting in damage to their reputation.

Media Influence and the Magnification Effect:
Scandals involving the Royal Family are exacerbated by the power and reach of the media. The constant presence of tabloids, social media, and broadcast news outlets amplifies the impact of scandals on public perception. The media, often driven by the pursuit of sensationalism and controversy, has the ability to magnify these scandals, making them seem more significant than they may be in reality. This media attention fuels public debate and shapes public opinion, leading to a potential erosion of trust and a negative impact on the reputation of the Royal Family.

Handling Scandals and Recovering Reputation:
The Royal Family's ability to effectively handle scandals plays a crucial role in maintaining their reputation. An effective response can mitigate the negative impact, protecting the monarchy from further damage. Transparency, honesty, and accountability are key principles that must be upheld during times of scandal. Acknowledging mistakes, taking responsibility, and visibly working toward resolution are essential steps in rebuilding public trust.

Furthermore, the Royal Family must adapt to changing societal expectations. Times of scandal often challenge long-standing traditions and highlight the need for modernization. By addressing public concerns, promoting transparency, and embracing progressive values, the Royal Family can regain public confidence and protect their reputation from further harm.

Scandals have undeniably played a significant role in shaping the reputation of the Royal Family. Personal and financial improprieties, intensified by media attention, have the potential to damage public trust and perpetuate negative perceptions. However, the Royal Family's ability to handle these scandals, exemplify transparency, and adapt to societal changes is crucial in restoring and maintaining their reputation.

As the world continues to evolve, the Royal Family's reputation will continue to be shaped by scandals and public opinion. By learning from past experiences and proactively addressing potential controversies, the Royal Family can strive to maintain a positive image and ensure the continued support and admiration of the public. Ultimately, their reputation rests on their commitment to transparency, ethical conduct, and responsiveness to public expectations over time.

How the monarchy has adapted to changing attitudes

In this discourse, we will explore how the monarchy has skillfully adapted to changing attitudes throughout history to maintain its relevance and support from the people. From the constitutional monarchy concept to embracing modern values, we will delve into the various ways in which the monarchy has evolved and endeavored to connect with the changing aspirations and expectations of society.

Understanding Shifting Perceptions:
To comprehend the monarchy's adaptability, we must first acknowledge the changing attitudes prevalent in society. With the advent of democracy and the rise of egalitarian ideals, traditional notions of absolute power have gradually been replaced with a more ceremonial role for monarchs. As people yearned for greater political participation and equality, it became imperative for the monarchy to reflect these shifting perspectives while preserving its symbolic significance. This led to a profound transformation in the way the monarchy interacts with its subjects.

Constitutional Monarchy: Balancing Tradition and Modernity:
One significant milestone in the monarchy's adaptation was the establishment of constitutional monarchy systems. Countries such as the United Kingdom, Sweden, and Japan embraced this model, which shared power between the monarchy and elected representatives. Constitutional monarchies ensured that the monarchy's role became predominantly ceremonial, assuaging concerns about excessive influence while still maintaining a vital link to the nation's history and traditions. By accepting a limited role, monarchs demonstrated their willingness to adapt to democratic principles while also acknowledging the changing aspirations of their people.

Modernizing the Monarchy's Image:
Another adaptation employed by the monarchy was

modernizing its image to resonate with contemporary society. Recognizing the importance of relatability and accessibility, monarchs began to engage with their subjects more openly. With the advent of mass media, they embraced new communication channels to create a more approachable and friendly persona. Queen Elizabeth II, for example, initiated televised Christmas messages in 1957, allowing her to directly address the nation and forge a personal connection with her subjects. Similarly, the monarchy actively participated in the digital era, utilizing social media platforms to engage with a broader audience and adapt to the changing communication landscape.

Embracing Cultural and Social Progress:
As attitudes towards cultural and social issues evolved, the monarchy faced the challenge of keeping pace with these changes. Monarchs recognized the importance of supporting diversity, inclusivity, and social progress, and made conscious efforts to champion causes and initiatives aligned with the shifting societal narrative. For instance, in recent years, the British royal family has actively addressed mental health issues through the Heads Together campaign, highlighting their commitment to destigmatizing mental health struggles and promoting emotional well-being. By embracing such causes, the monarchy has demonstrated its adaptability to contemporary concerns and has sought to remain connected to its subjects.

Maintaining Relevance through Philanthropy and Diplomacy:
To ensure relevance, the monarchy has strategically aligned itself with charitable pursuits and diplomatic efforts. Monarchs and their families consistently engage in philanthropic activities, using their status and influence to positively impact society. By supporting charitable causes, initiatives, and organizations, the monarchy demonstrates its commitment to addressing societal needs and contributes to the betterment of communities. Additionally, through diplomatic endeavors, monarchs actively cultivate relationships with other nations, showcasing the relevance and value they bring to international diplomacy.

Despite the changing attitudes and societal shifts over time, the monarchy has shown remarkable adaptability and resilience. By accepting constitutional limitations, modernizing their image, embracing cultural and social progress, and engaging in philanthropy and diplomacy, monarchs and royal families have remained connected to their subjects while also fulfilling a relevant role in the modern era. The ability of the monarchy to adapt to evolving attitudes has undoubtedly contributed to its enduring place in many nations' hearts and histories, ensuring its continued relevance and support from the public.

Chapter 9: Royal Traditions and Ceremonies

The coronation ceremony

The roots of coronation ceremonies can be traced back to ancient times, when kings and queens would ascend to their positions through a divine right. In many cultures, these rituals were believed to bestow legitimacy upon the ruler, solidifying their position as a representative of their deity or deity. Over the centuries, coronations have evolved and adapted to reflect the changing political and social landscapes, but their core purpose remains intact – to publicly proclaim and affirm the new monarch's authority.

One of the most defining aspects of a coronation is its pageantry. From the grand processions to the regal attire worn by the monarch, every detail is carefully choreographed to showcase the majesty and significance of the occasion. The ceremony often takes place in a majestic venue, such as a cathedral or palace, adding to the overall spectacle and awe-inspiring atmosphere. The royal regalia, including the crown and scepter, are symbolic representations of power and serve to visually reinforce the authority of the newly crowned monarch.

Equally important in a coronation ceremony is the religious element. In many monarchies, the monarch derives their authority from divine sanction, and the coronation serves as a public affirmation of this connection. The head of the church, be it a bishop, archbishop, or even a pope, may play a central role in the ceremony, anointing the monarch with holy oil and offering blessings. This union of religious and secular power is a longstanding tradition that underscores the unique relationship between monarchs and their religious subjects.

Throughout history, coronations have also been occasions for the reaffirmation of social contracts between the ruler and the people. The monarch takes oaths and promises to uphold the rights, laws, and customs of the realm, while the subjects pledge their allegiance and loyalty to the sovereign. These promises provide a formal framework for the relationship between the ruler and the governed, emphasizing the mutual responsibilities and obligations that exist within a monarchy. While the specifics of these oaths may differ from country to country, they generally serve to remind both parties of their respective roles and duties.

Although coronations have a rich and storied history, questions have been raised about their relevance in today's modern world. In nations where monarchies have transitioned to constitutional monarchies, the role of the monarch has shifted from a governing position to a ceremonial and symbolic one. Nevertheless, coronations continue to be important ceremonial events, imbued with historical and cultural significance. They provide an opportunity for national unity, celebrating a shared heritage and identity that transcends politics and divides.

In recent times, the media has played a vital role in making coronation ceremonies accessible to a global audience. Live broadcasts and extensive coverage allow people from all corners of the world to witness these historical moments. The modernization of communication technology has transformed coronations into inclusive events, fostering a sense of collective celebration across borders. This globalization of the coronation experience ensures that these ceremonies remain relevant and continue to captivate the imagination of millions. They are profound demonstrations of power, tradition, and unity, offering glimpses into the past while shaping the future. Unlike other events, coronations are steeped in symbolism, both religious and cultural, and bring together elements of pageantry and spectacle that captivate and inspire. As the world evolves, so do coronations, adapting to changing times while preserving their intrinsic value. These ceremonies represent a bridge between the regal past and the modern-day, reminding us of the enduring legacy of monarchy.

State occasions such as Trooping the Colour

The roots of Trooping the Colour can be traced back to the 17th century when military units began "trooping" their regimental colors. These colorful flags served as rallying points for soldiers during battle, helping to maintain unity and cohesion. Over time, the act of trooping the colors became associated with the monarch's birthday, evolving into the elaborate spectacle we witness today. The ceremony underwent various changes and formalizations throughout the centuries, finally finding its current form during the reign of Queen Victoria, whose steadfast commitment to ceremonial traditions shaped the modern monarchy.

The centerpiece of Trooping the Colour is the Royal Procession, wherein Her Majesty, accompanied by other members of the royal family, rides in a horse-drawn carriage from Buckingham Palace to Horse Guards Parade. This majestic display highlights the continuity of the monarchy and its role as a unifying force within the nation. The Queen's Guards, resplendent in their scarlet tunics and bearskin hats, form an impressive escort, representing centuries of military tradition and solidarity. Crowds gather along the Mall, joyously waving flags and cheering, creating an atmosphere of celebration and patriotism.

As the royal party arrives at Horse Guards Parade, the Trooping the Colour ceremony begins with a musical accompaniment by the Massed Bands of the Household Division. The sound of music fills the air, entrancing spectators and adding further grandeur to the occasion. The ceremony itself is a meticulously choreographed affair, featuring a display of precision marching and drill movements by the Foot Guards. This showcase of military discipline pays homage to the deep connection between the British monarchy and its armed forces, highlighting their shared history and mutual respect.

However, Trooping the Colour is not merely a historic reenactment. It serves as a potent symbol of national unity and pride, reflecting the modern values of the United Kingdom. The diversity of the armed forces is prominently showcased, with regiments from various backgrounds and cultures participating in the ceremony. This inclusivity sends a powerful message of unity and equality, demonstrating the nation's commitment to diversity and multiculturalism. Trooping the Colour acts as a reminder of the strength and togetherness of the British people, transcending class, ethnicity, and individual differences.

Beyond its cultural and symbolic significance, Trooping the Colour also has practical implications. The ceremony provides an opportunity for the training and evaluation of the Foot Guards, ensuring their readiness to carry out ceremonial duties and military operations. The intricate drill movements and synchronized displays serve as displays of the Guards' discipline, teamwork, and professionalism. These skills, honed through regular practice and preparation, are vital in upholding the reputation and prestige of the British military.

Trooping the Colour is an event that captivates both locals and visitors, drawing millions of spectators each year. It has become an integral part of British cultural identity, with families and communities coming together to witness and celebrate their shared heritage. The celebratory atmosphere extends beyond the parade ground, with street parties, concerts, and festivities taking place across the country. Trooping the Colour unites the nation, fostering a sense of belonging and camaraderie among its people.

In the digital age, Trooping the Colour has also embraced new technologies to expand its reach and engage with a wider audience. The ceremony is broadcasted on television and streamed online, enabling people from all corners of the globe to experience the grandeur and elegance of the event. Social media platforms further amplify the occasion, with hashtags and live updates turning Trooping the Colour into a global conversation. This modernization ensures that the traditions and values upheld by Trooping the Colour continue to resonate with present and future generations. This grand state occasion not only commemorates the monarch's official birthday but also serves as a powerful symbol of national unity, pride, and inclusivity. The ceremony's magnificent displays, precision marching, and musical accompaniment captivate audiences and evoke a sense of awe and admiration. Trooping the Colour is not merely a relic of the past; it is a living tradition that adapts to the changing times, bringing people together and fostering a shared sense of belonging.

The role of the Royal Family in national life

The presence of a monarch has not only been a constant throughout the nation's past, but it has also played a significant role in shaping its present and future. This comprehensive exploration aims to shed light on the multifaceted role of the Royal Family in national life, exploring the ways in which they foster unity, provide stability, and serve as symbols of continuity and national pride.

1. Unifying the Nation:
While modern Britain is notably diverse in terms of culture, religion, and political views, the Royal Family plays a crucial role in unifying the nation. Regardless of personal beliefs or backgrounds, British citizens often find a sense of collective identity and loyalty in their shared allegiance to the monarchy. This unifying effect is particularly evident during national events, such as jubilees, weddings, or state visits, where people come together in celebration or support of the royal institution. The Royal Family's ability to bring people from diverse backgrounds together helps to create a sense of unity and pride in being British.

2. Symbolic Representation:
The Royal Family serves as a powerful symbol of national identity, representing the values, traditions, and history of the British people. The Crown, embodied by the reigning monarch, stands as a physical embodiment of the nation and its sovereignty. The Queen, as the head of state, carries out ceremonial duties that symbolize continuity and resilience in the face of change. In addition, the Royal Family acts as influential emissaries on the world stage, promoting British culture, diplomacy, and forging international relationships, ultimately enhancing the nation's global standing.

3. Preserving Tradition and History:
British history is closely intertwined with its monarchy. The Royal Family, through their continuous presence over centuries, embodies and preserves the traditions and heritage that are intrinsic to the nation's identity. The monarchy acts as a living connection to the past, securing a sense of stability and continuity in an ever-changing world. Ceremonies such as the State Opening of Parliament, Trooping the Colour, or the Changing of the Guard provide a tangible link to centuries-old rituals, reinforcing the historical fabric of the nation and keeping traditions alive for future generations.

4. Promoting Charitable Work:
Beyond their ceremonial duties, members of the Royal Family

play a crucial role as patrons of numerous charitable organizations, making substantial contributions to various social causes. The Royal Family's involvement in philanthropy brings visibility and support to local communities throughout the country, amplifying public awareness and driving positive change. Their patronage ensures that these organizations receive the necessary attention and resources to address a wide range of issues, from healthcare and education to wildlife conservation and mental health.

5. Influencing Public Discourse:
While the Queen and other members of the Royal Family are expected to remain politically neutral, they possess a unique ability to influence public discourse in significant and subtle ways. Through their speeches, public appearances, and interactions with people from all walks of life, they offer a moral compass and provide a sense of shared values amidst divisive societal debates. Their dedication to public service and empathy for the concerns of citizens serve as a source of comfort and inspiration, allowing their words and actions to resonate with the population at large.

The role of the Royal Family in national life is far from simple or one-dimensional. Instead, it encompasses a spectrum of functions, blending tradition, symbolism, unity, and service. Their ability to foster unity, preserve tradition, embody national identity, and contribute to the greater good has allowed the monarchy to retain its relevance in the ever-changing landscape of modern society. As Britain navigates through the challenges of the future, the role of the Royal Family remains a steadfast source of stability, continuity, and national pride.

Chapter 10: Conclusion

The enduring fascination with royalty

The fascination with royalty has captivated societies for centuries, and it endures as a subject of intrigue and wonder even in the modern world. From the majestic splendor of ancient monarchies to the contemporary lives of reigning kings and queens, the allure of royalty transcends generations and cultures. This enduring fascination is evident in various forms, such as the popularity of royal weddings, the fascination with royal scandals, and the enduring interest in royal history. In this book, we aim to explore the reasons behind this enduring fascination with royalty, shedding light on the psychological, sociocultural, and historical factors that contribute to our fascination with kings and queens.

The Psychological Appeal

In examining the enduring fascination with royalty, it is important to consider its psychological appeal. Royalty embodies power, wealth, and grandeur, which resonate deeply with our innate desire for security, significance, and adulation. The charisma and aura surrounding royalty appeal to our fantasies of a life filled with opulence and influence. The royal symbol, be it a crown or a regal residence, represents stability and tradition, giving us a sense of continuity in a rapidly changing world. Additionally, the concept of a monarch being born into their position highlights an aspect of destiny and fate, which intrigues our imaginations.

The Sociocultural Influence

Beyond the psychological appeal, the enduring fascination with royalty also stems from sociocultural factors ingrained within our societies. Throughout history, royalty has played a central role in societal structures, acting as figureheads for nations. The pomp and circumstance associated with royal ceremonies and events capture our attention and create a sense of spectacle and grandeur. These rituals and traditions provide a shared cultural experience that transcends generations, creating a sense of national identity and pride. This sociocultural influence further reinforces our fascination with royalty and deepens our emotional connection with it.

Historical Context

A significant aspect of the enduring fascination with royalty lies in historical context. Kings and queens have shaped the course of history, having influenced politics, culture, and society. Their reigns are often marked by significant events that have changed the world we live in. The lives and actions of historical monarchs are a source of inspiration and intrigue, providing valuable insights into our own past. Exploring the lives of iconic figures such as Queen Elizabeth I, Louis XIV, or Cleopatra not only offers historical knowledge but also engenders an admiration for their ability to navigate complex political landscapes and leave a lasting legacy.

Celebrity Culture and Media Influence

In the contemporary era, the fascination with royalty has been further propelled by the rise of celebrity culture and media influence. The lives of modern-day royals are played out under public scrutiny, chronicled in tabloids, and showcased through various media platforms. This continuous stream of information and imagery amplifies our fascination with their seemingly glamorous and extraordinary lives. The presence of royalty in popular culture, from movies and TV shows to fashion and lifestyle magazines, ensures that we are constantly exposed to their allure.

Identification and Escape

Our enduring fascination with royalty is also rooted in our desire for identification and escape. Monarchs serve as archetypal figures, representing ideals of power, grace, and elegance. They embody qualities that many of us aspire to possess, allowing us to project ourselves onto their narratives. Escaping into the world of royalty, whether through historical accounts or contemporary media, offers respite from the challenges and mundane realities of our own lives. It allows us to dream, untethered by the constraints of our social standing and limitations.

The allure of royalty, be it historical or modern, continues to captivate and fascinate us. The psychological appeal, sociocultural influence, historical context, celebrity culture, and our own desire for identification and escape all contribute to this enduring fascination. Exploring this multifaceted phenomenon allows us to gain insights into our collective imagination and the human condition. Understanding why we are drawn to royalty helps us appreciate the significance of their presence in our societies, contributing both to our cultural heritage and our ongoing journey of self-discovery.

Final thoughts on the Royal Family Tree and its place in history

Throughout history, the Royal Family Tree has played a significant role in shaping the course of nations and historical events. As we conclude our journey into the intricate web of relationships and bloodlines that constitute this illustrious family, it is essential to reflect on the importance and relevance of their place in history. The Royal Family Tree is not merely a collection of names and lineages; it represents the very essence of monarchy, power, and tradition. While some may argue that it is an archaic institution, it cannot be denied that the monarchy continues to captivate the imagination of people worldwide.

One of the most compelling aspects of the Royal Family Tree is the sense of continuity it provides. Through centuries of change, upheaval, and political transformations, the monarchy has endured, acting as a unifying force for nations. The Royal Family, with its lineage stretching back generations, offers a tangible connection to the past that fosters a sense of stability and tradition. It is through this family tree that we can trace the origins and development of British monarchy, observing the intricate interplay between dynastic ambitions, power struggles, and the shaping of national identity.

Another significant aspect of the Royal Family Tree is its portrayal of the familial bonds that permeate both their public and private lives. As we follow the branches and connections within the tree, we gain insight into the personal relationships and family dynamics that have influenced the fate of nations.

From great triumphs to terrible tragedies, the Royal Family Tree has borne witness to it all. By studying their interconnectedness, we not only gain a greater understanding of their place in history but also humanize these iconic figures, making their stories relatable and accessible to a broader audience.

Moreover, the Royal Family Tree serves as a window into a bygone era, allowing us to explore the customs, traditions, and values that have shaped the monarchy. By examining the ancestral roots of the monarchy, we can start to comprehend the foundation upon which British society and governance were built. From the feudal system to the establishment of constitutional monarchy, the Royal Family Tree serves as a living record of the evolution of political systems and societal norms. It offers a glimpse into the lives of kings and queens, princes and princesses, whose duty to serve their nation has often been intertwined with personal desires and ambitions.

While the Royal Family Tree may hold importance on a national level, its significance can be felt well beyond the British shores. Monarchies across the globe have often looked to the British Royal Family as a blueprint for their own monarchic institutions. The sight of the Queen, her family, and their interactions during state visits, ceremonial occasions, and public appearances symbolizes the enduring relevance and appeal of the monarchy as an institution. The Royal Family Tree is instrumental in solidifying diplomatic ties and fostering relationships between nations, acting as cultural ambassadors for the British people.

However, it is essential to acknowledge the evolving nature of the monarchy and its place in contemporary society. The Royal Family Tree, with its intricate lineage and strict rules of succession, operates within a framework that is at times seen as outdated and non-inclusive. As society progresses and embraces more diverse perspectives, there is an increasing call for the monarchy to adapt and reflect the changing dynamics of modern Britain. This challenge presents an opportunity for the Royal Family to redefine their role and relevance, ensuring that they remain connected to the aspirations and expectations of the people they serve. It gives us insight into the continuity, familial bonds, and traditions that characterize monarchy, while also serving as a living record of the evolution of political systems and societal norms. Beyond its national significance, the Royal Family Tree acts as a cultural touchstone that resonates with people worldwide, symbolizing the timeless allure of the monarchy. As we bid farewell to our exploration of this rich and intricate lineage, let us remember that while the Royal Family Tree may have its roots in the past, its branches extend ever forward, carrying with them the hopes and aspirations of future generations.

Printed in Dunstable, United Kingdom